I SPY IN MY COMMUNITY

Alicia Rodriguez

# FARM

## A Crabtree Roots Book

Crabtree Publishing
crabtreebooks.com

# School-to-Home Support for Caregivers and Teachers

This book helps children grow by letting them practice reading. Here are a few guiding questions to help the reader with building his or her comprehension skills. Possible answers appear here in red.

## Before Reading:

- What do I think this book is about?
    - *I think this book is about what you can see on a farm.*
    - *I think this book is about different kinds of farms.*
- What do I want to learn about this topic?
    - *I want to learn what kinds of animals are on farms.*
    - *I want to learn what a farm looks like.*

## During Reading:

- I wonder why...
    - *I wonder why corn plants grow in rows.*
    - *I wonder why farmers use tractors.*
- What have I learned so far?
    - *I have learned that crops grow in fields.*
    - *I have learned that chickens lay eggs on farms.*

## After Reading:

- What details did I learn about this topic?
    - *I have learned that farmers use tractors.*
    - *I have learned that there are a lot of things to see on farms.*
- Read the book again and look for the vocabulary words.
    - *I see the word **field** on page 8 and the word **tractor** on page 10. The other vocabulary words are found on page 14.*

Let's take a walk around the farm.

The cows give milk.

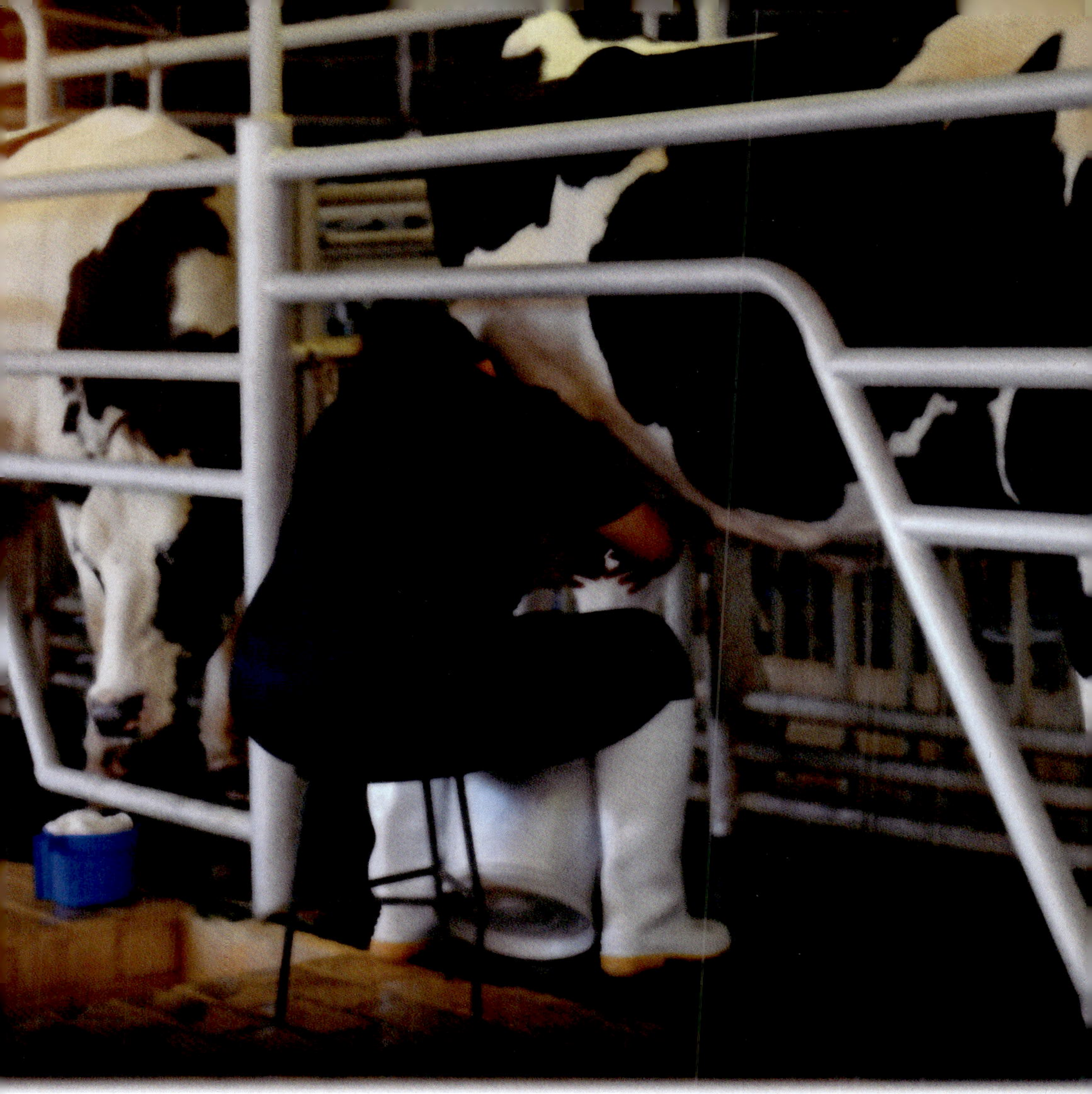

The chickens lay eggs.

Look at the corn
in the **field.**

There are **tomato plants**, too.

The farmer uses a **tractor**.

Workers pick
the **crops.**

There is so much to see at the farm!

# Word List

## Sight Words

a
are
around
at
chickens
corn
cows
eggs
farm
give
in
let's
look
milk
much
pick
see
so
take
the
there
to
too
walk
workers

## Words to Know

crops

field

tomato plants

tractor

# 45 Words

Let's take a walk around the farm.

The cows give milk.

The chickens lay eggs.

Look at the corn in the **field**.

There are **tomato plants**, too.

The farmer uses a **tractor**.

Workers pick the **crops**.

There is so much to see at the farm!

# Crabtree Publishing

crabtreebooks.com 800-387-7650



In Canada: We acknowledge the financial support of the Government of Canada through the Canada Book Fund for our publishing activities.

| | |
|---|---|
| Hardcover | 978-1-4271-5724-9 |
| Paperback | 978-1-4271-5730-0 |
| Ebook (pdf) | 978-1-4271-3370-0 |
| Epub | 978-1-4271-3430-1 |
| Read-along | 978-1-4271-5748-5 |
| Audio book | 978-1-4271-5754-6 |

**Library and Archives Canada Cataloguing in Publication**

Title: Farm / Alicia Rodriguez.
Names: Rodriguez, Alicia (Children's author), author.
Description: Series statement: I spy in my community | "A Crabtree roots book".
Identifiers: Canadiana (print) 2021019748X | Canadiana (ebook) 20210197498 | ISBN 9781427157249 (hardcover) | ISBN 9781427157300 (softcover) | ISBN 9781427133700 (HTML) | ISBN 9781427134301 (EPUB) | ISBN 9781427157485 (read-along ebook)
Subjects: LCSH: Farms—Juvenile literature.
Classification: LCC S519 .R63 2022 | DDC j630—dc23

Printed in Canada/042024/CP20240429

**Published in Canada**
**Crabtree Publishing**
616 Welland Avenue
St. Catharines, Ontario
L2M 5V6

**Published in the United States**
**Crabtree Publishing**
347 Fifth Avenue
Suite 1402-145
New York, NY 10016

Written by: Alicia Rodriguez
Designed by: Rhea Wallace
Series Development: James Earley
Proofreader: Janine Deschenes
Educational Consultant: Marie Lemke M.Ed.
Photographs: Shutterstock: David Orcea: cover (top left); Layue: cover (top right); MaxyM: cover (bottom); Fred Cardoso: p. 3; Yanawut.S: p. 4-5; Matusciac Alexandru: p. 8, 14; Fotokostic: p. 9, 14; Vevchic: p. 10, 14; Spain: p. 11, 14; SGR: p. 13

**Library of Congress Cataloging-in-Publication Data**

Names: Rodriguez, Alicia (Children's author) author.
Title: Farm / Alicia Rodriguez.
Description: New York, NY : Crabtree Publishing, 2022. | Series: I spy in my community - A Crabtree Roots boo | Includes index.
Identifiers: LCCN 2021018049 (print) | LCCN 2021018050 (ebook) | ISBN 9781427157249 (hardcover) | ISBN 9781427157300 (paperback) | ISBN 9781427133700 (ebook) | ISBN 9781427134301 (epub) | ISBN 9781427157485
Subjects: LCSH: Farmers--Juvenile literature. | Agriculture--Juvenile literature.
Classification: LCC HD8039.F3 R63 2022 (print) | LCC HD8039.F3 (ebook) | DDC 338.1--dc23
LC record available at https://lccn.loc.gov/2021018049
LC ebook record available at https://lccn.loc.gov/2021018050